This book

belongs to

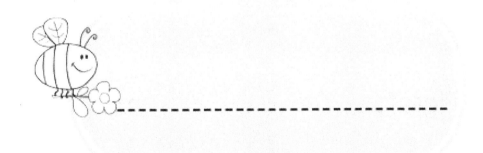

Spain - English

billetera

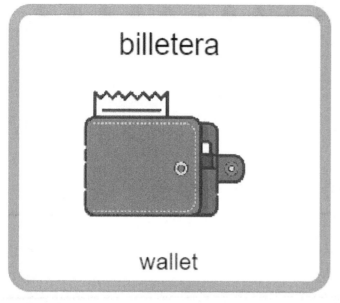

wallet

trabajando

working

lagartija

lizard

orgulloso

proud

bolígrafo

pen

mofetas

skunk

gorila

gorilla

debajo

under

hexágono

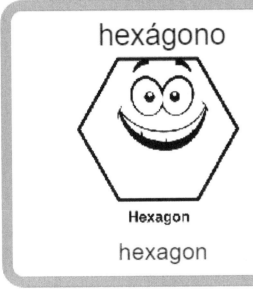

Hexagon

hexagon

cremallera

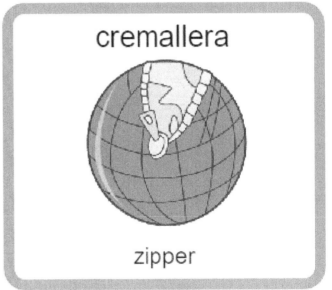

zipper

ramo de flores

bouquet

meneo

wag

puente

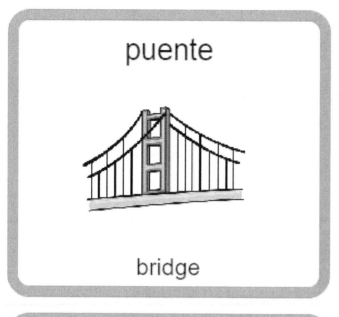

bridge

máscara

mask

equipo

team

barril

barrel

los males

evil

adiós

goodbye

familia

family

filete

steak

motor

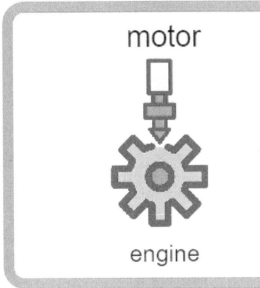

engine

abierto

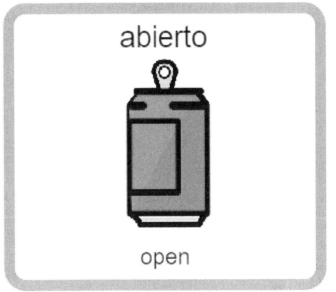

open

leche

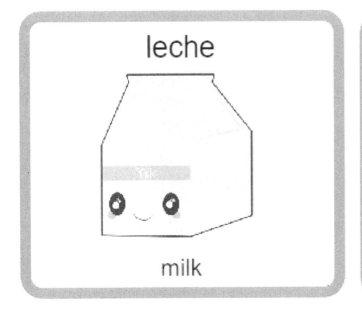

milk

jamón

ham

barba

beard

béisbol

baseball

caimán

alligator

caliente

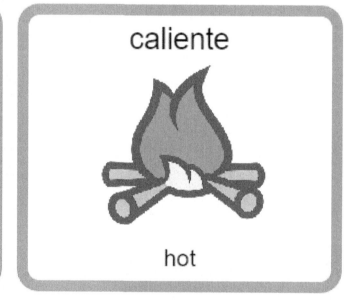

hot

músculo

muscle

rojo

red

canción

song

cortinas

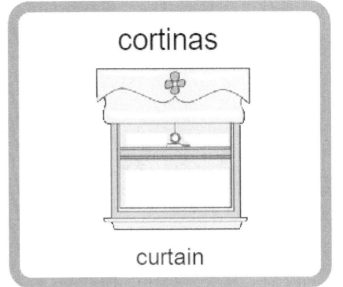

curtain

malo

bad

cama

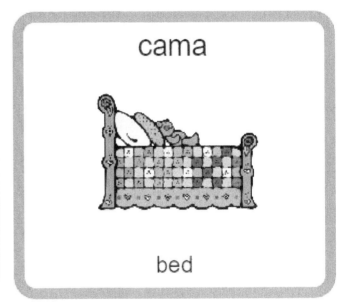

bed

anillo

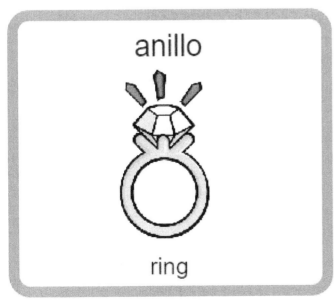

ring

copo de nieve

snowflake

niños

children

cocina

kitchen

hermana

sister

fantasmas

ghost

puntos

point

arete

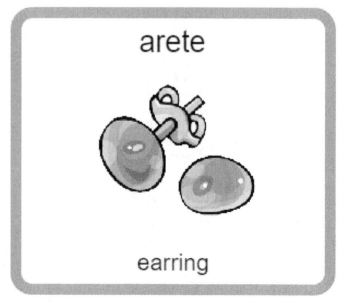

earring

dado

dice

agresivo

aggressive

simpático

friendly

medicación

medication

madre

mother

almohada

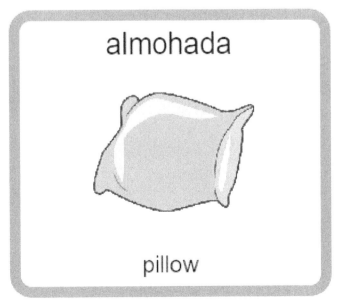

pillow

dibujo

drawing

danza

dance

almeja

clam

melocotón

peach

perro

dog

shorts

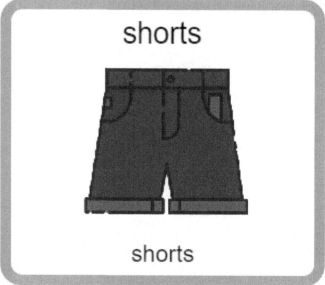

shorts

equitación

riding

medias

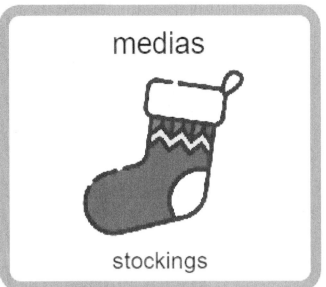

stockings

navidad

christmas

semillas

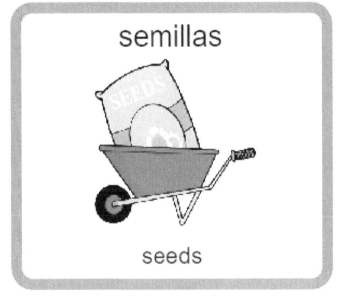

seeds

chile

chili

llorar

cry

masajes

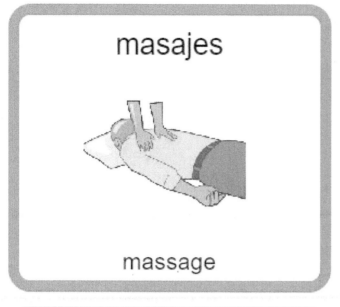

massage

ciervo

deer

mano

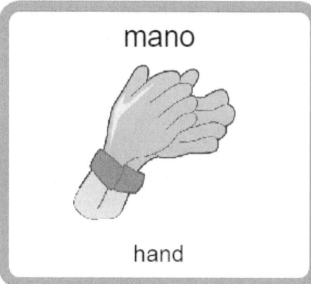

hand

cuatro

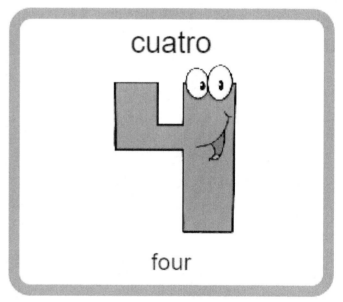

four

pan

pan

la marmota

groundhog

alfiler

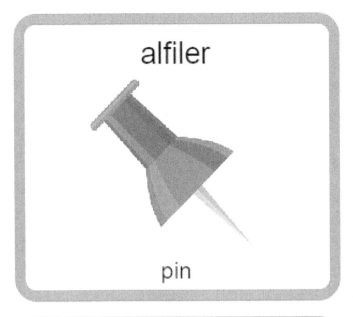

pin

dinero

money

pudín

pudding

plátano

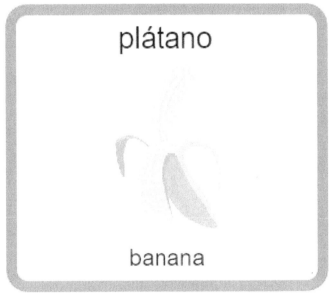

banana

uno

one

carpintero

carpenter

escritorios

desk

brujas

witch

hormiga

ant

abrazo

hug

bandeja

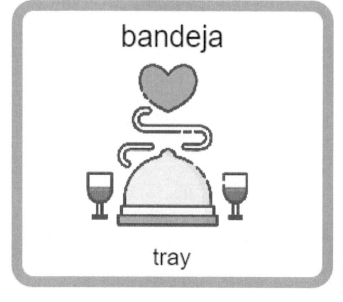

tray

fresa

strawberry

salsa de tomate

ketchup

araña

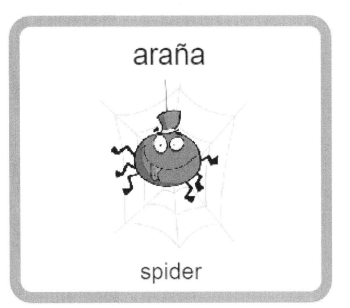

spider

podio

podium

charco

puddle

alpinismo

climbing

caja

box

tintas

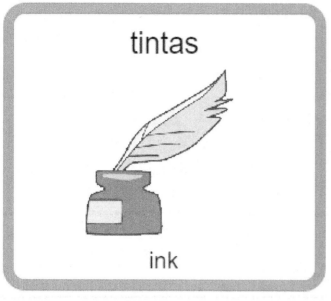

ink

hipopótamo

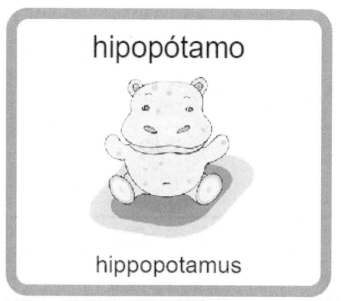

hippopotamus

rosquillas

donut

suelo

soil

capa

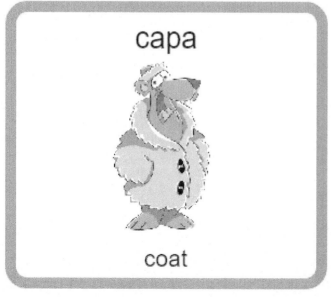

coat

carrera

race

cinturón

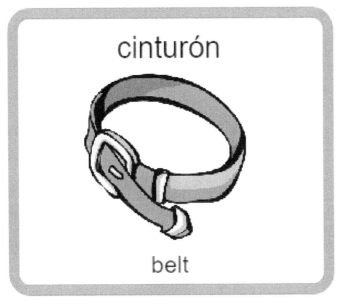

belt

horno

oven

barbero

barber

rebanar

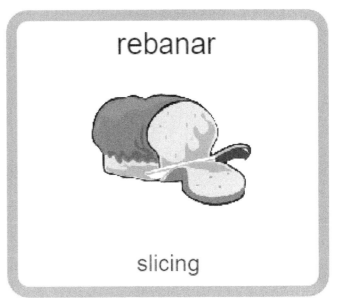

slicing

chimenea

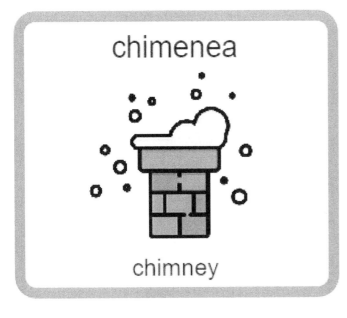

chimney

vacuna

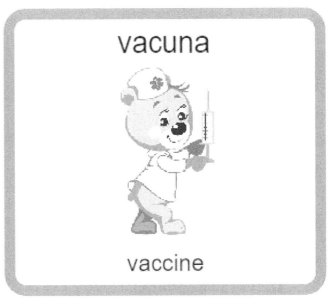

vaccine

café

coffee

hoja

leaf

elegante

stylish

esteras

mat

caballo

horse

motos

scooter

taxi

cab

tiburón

shark

bombas

bomb

alfombras

rug

playa

beach

feliz

happy

pizza

pizza

calendario
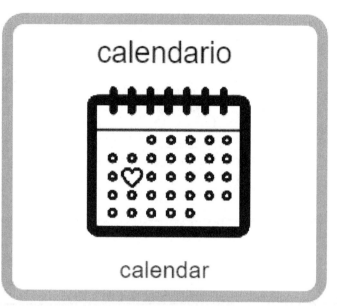
calendar

hielo

ice

diez

ten

pizarra

chalkboard

boca

mouth

sandía

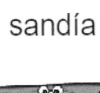

watermelon

micrófono

microphone

carta

letter

abeja

bee

hotel

hotel

calle

street

caramelo

candy

mamá

mom

avión

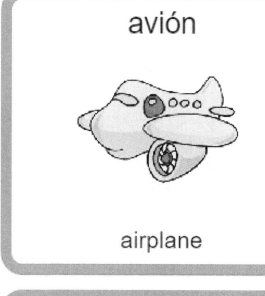

airplane

brócoli

broccoli

casa

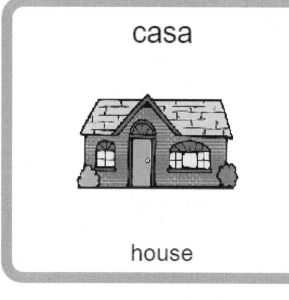

house

tambor

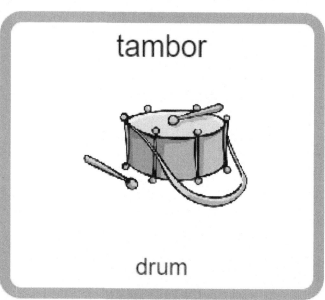

drum

velas

candle

erizo

hedgehog

mariposa

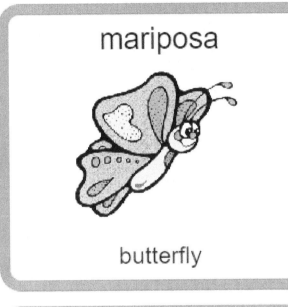

butterfly

impresionar

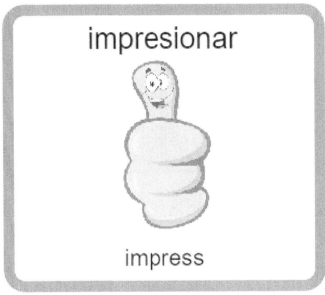

impress

muelle

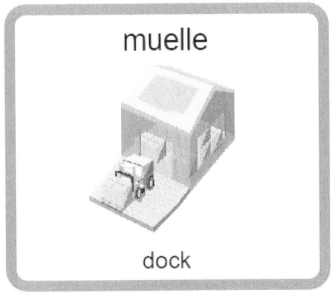

dock

estufa

stove

papel

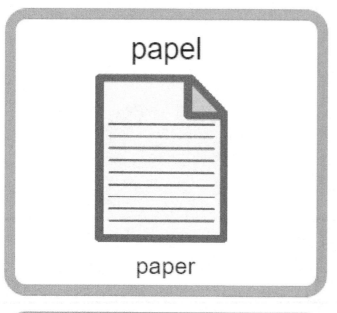

paper

levántate

stand up

lacarpa

tent

cuerpo

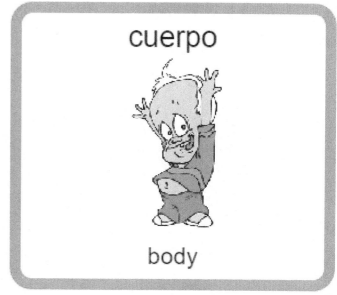

body

pijama

pajamas

trotar

jogging

utensilios

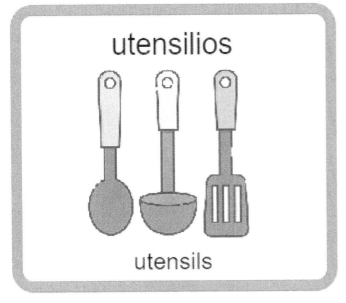

utensils

collar

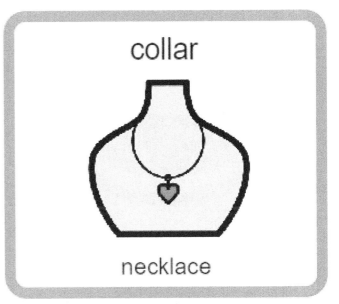

necklace

gallo

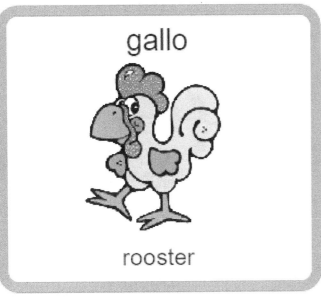

rooster

chícharos

peas

diamante

diamond

tumba

tombstone

galleta

cookie

casco
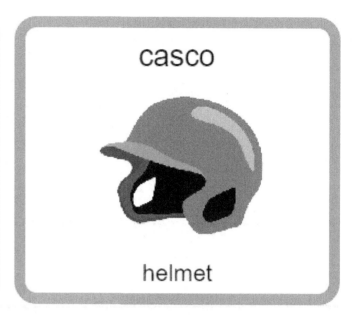
helmet

mandarina

tangerine

coche

car

cuna
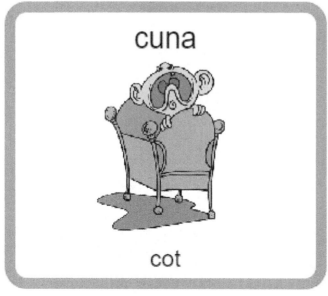
cot

pulgares

thumb

isla

island

chupetes

pacifier

lamparas

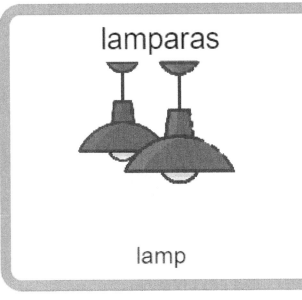

lamp

cámara

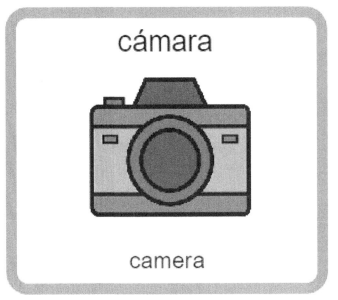

camera

pintar

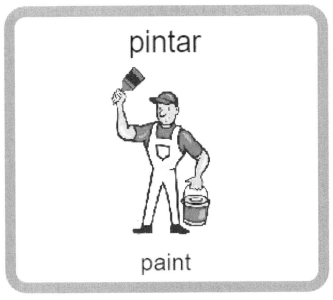

paint

violín

violin

tigre

tiger

música

music

reloj

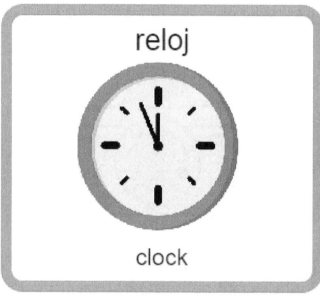

clock

estrella

star

jugar

play

suciedad

dirt

entrega

delivery

yegua

mare

ladrillo

brick

ganar

win

ocho

eight

libro

book

bandera

flag

cebra

zebra

pulpo

octopus

bicicleta

bicycle

moscas

fly

cereza

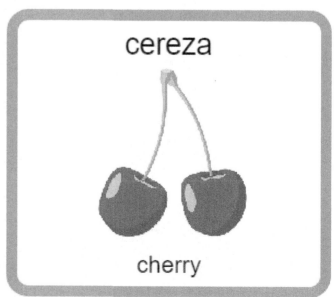

cherry

velero

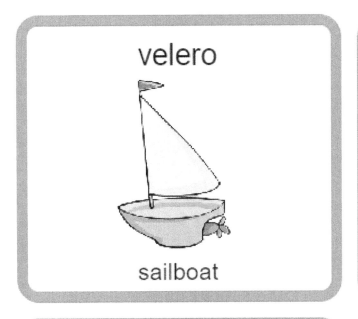

sailboat

trueno

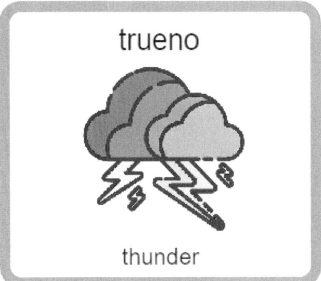

thunder

nueces

nut

pavo

turkey

conejo

rabbit

camisa

shirt

cadera

hip

pato

duck

reno

reindeer

servicio

serving

hacha

ax

amigo

friend

luna

moon

maletín

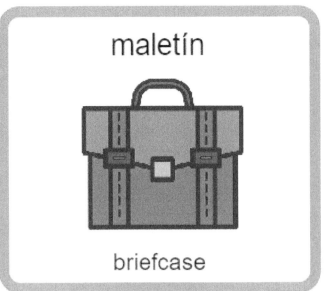

briefcase

colina

hill

jarra

jug

el respeto

respect

estudiando

studying

nueve

nine

codo

elbow

alimentación

feeding

celebrar

celebrate

noche

night

padre

father

piña

pineapple

nido

nest

calculadora

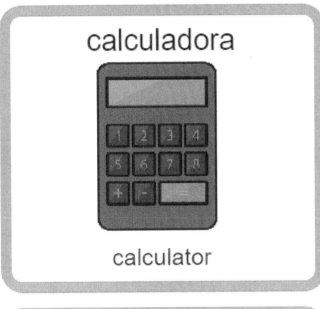

calculator

cohete

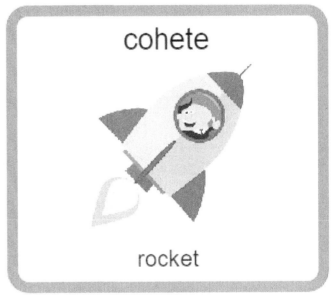

rocket

pirata

pirate

caras

face

mirando

looking

trenes

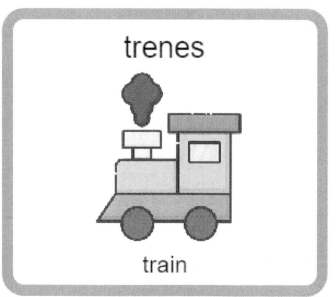

train

pez

fish

vaso

cup

mermelada

jam

delfín

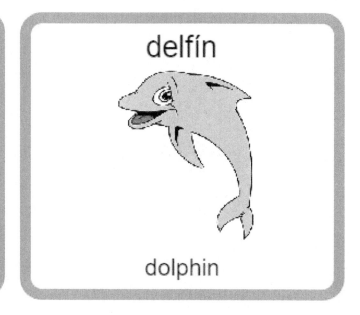

dolphin

enfermos

sick

mañana

morning

collares

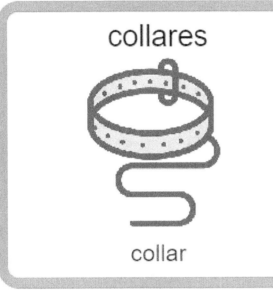

collar

pepino

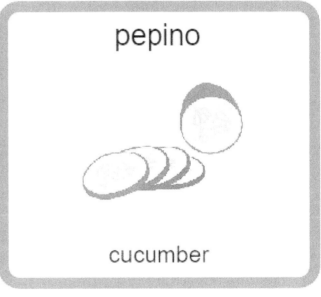

cucumber

trigo

wheat

jirafa

giraffe

insecto

bug

flechas
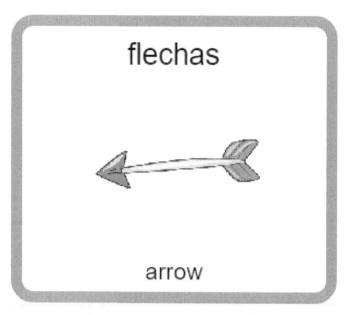
arrow

guitarra

guitar

artista

artist

taza para té

teacup

hombro

shoulder

herir

hurt

cerdo

pig

agua

water

zapatillas

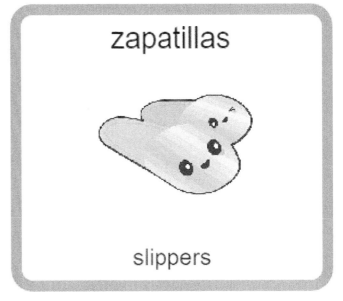

slippers

maní

peanut

granada

pomegranate

avestruz

ostrich

cesta

basket

lluvia

rain

pañuelo

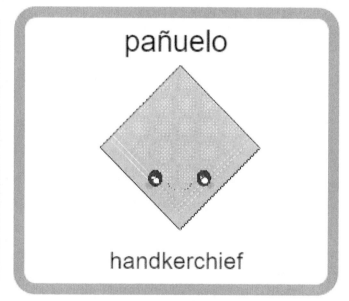

handkerchief

bellotas

acorn

saltar

jump

arrodillado

kneeling

soda

soda

estantería

bookshelf

manzana

apple

mendigar

beg

jardín

garden

raqueta

racket

gasolina

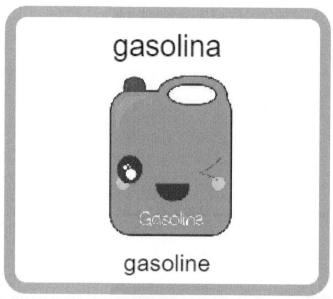

gasoline

saltando

hopping

palos

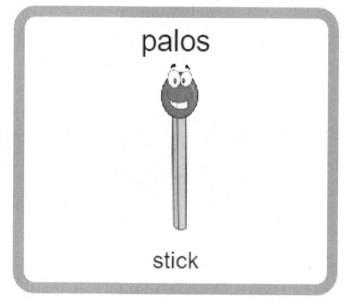

stick

colegio

school

partido

party

falda

skirt

arco iris

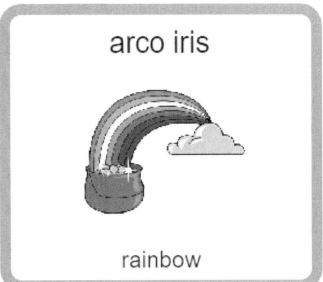

rainbow

niña

girl

ardillas

squirrel

tierra

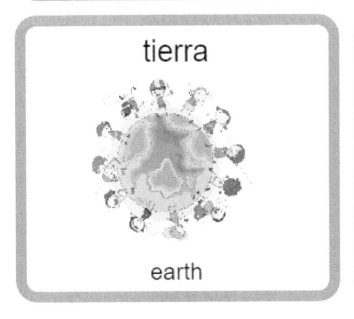

earth

linda

cute

suéteres

sweater

cangilón

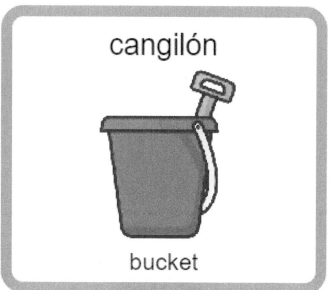

bucket

risa

laugh

jeeps

jeep

habitación

bedroom

baño

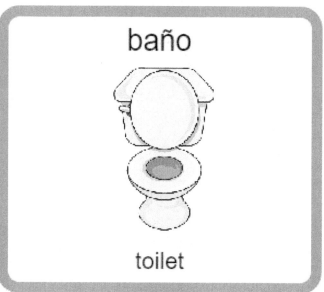

toilet

turbante

turban

golpear

hit

otoños

autumn

jugo

juice

cometa

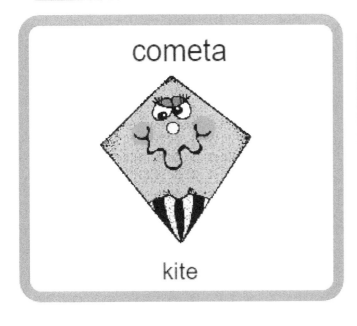

kite

hombre

man

cangrejo

crab

cocina

cooking

kiwi

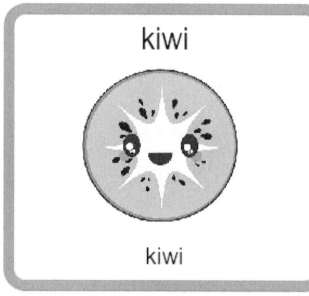

kiwi

gatito

kitten

espátula

spatula

té

tea

guirnalda

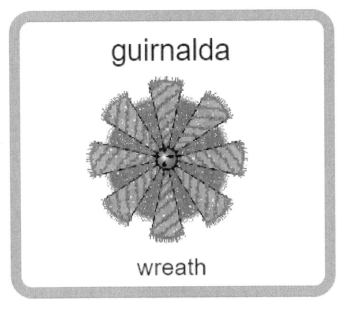

wreath

sonreír

smile

naranja

orange

números

number

mapas

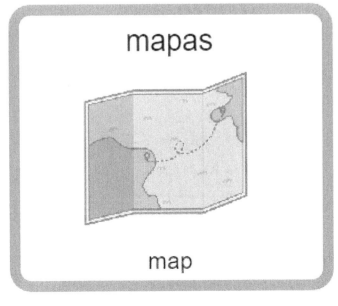

map

cena

dinner

rocas

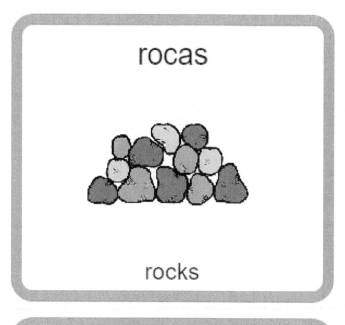

rocks

caminar

walk

edredones

quilt

buitre

vulture

rosa

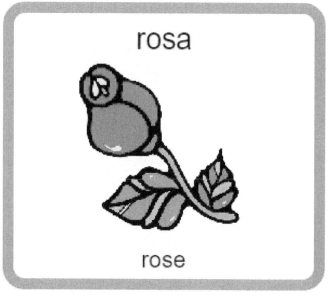

rose

gordo

fat

carne

meat

loto

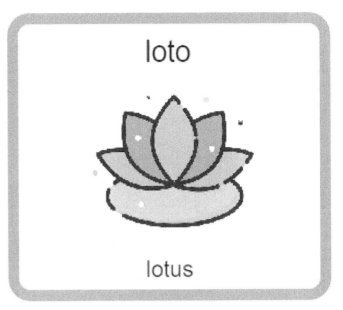

lotus

robar

rob

firma

signature

planchado

ironing

piano

piano

tranquilo

quiet

ensalada

salad

molino

windmill

ballena

whale

carnicero

butcher

topo

mole

grande

big

profesor

teacher

pelo

hair

sombrero

hat

apestoso

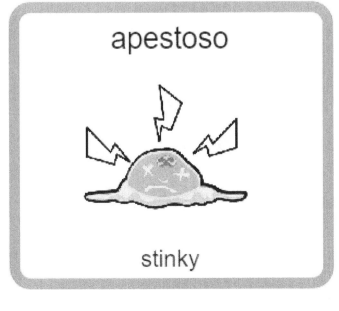

stinky

iguana

iguana

camareros

waiter

trapeadores

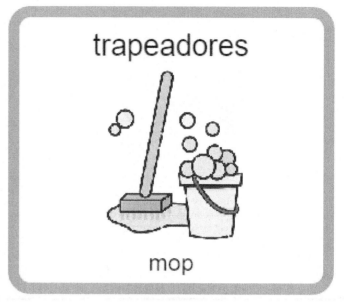

mop

telescopio

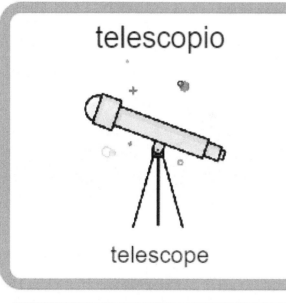

telescope

espejo

mirror

fuego

fire

escoba

broom

sacos

sack

paletas de hielo

popsicles

tracción

pulling

lobo

wolf

palma

palm

mancuernas

dumbbells

bufanda

scarf

florero

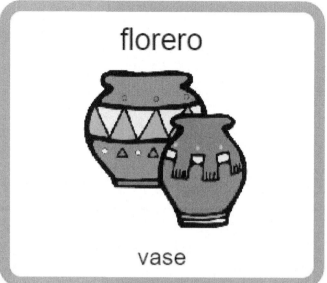

vase

hogar

fireplace

panadero

baker

bolso

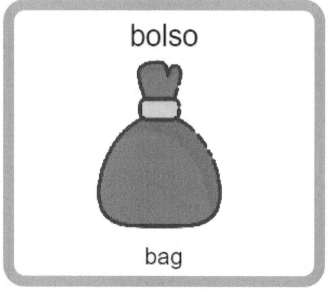

bag

ayuda

help

flor

flower

granja

farm

lápiz

pencil

calcetines

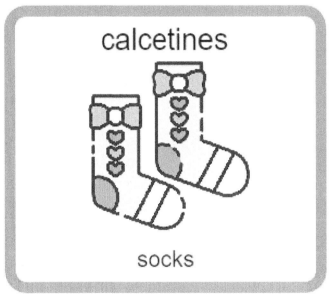

socks

líderes

leader

dormido

sleeping

bonita

pretty

ciruela

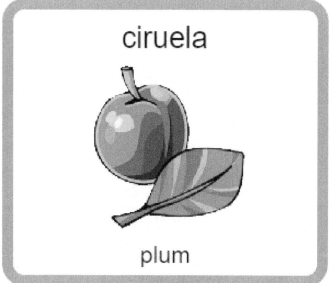

plum

juguete

toy

reina

queen

bañera

bathtub

enojado

angry

guepardo

cheetah

músico

musician

alfabetos

alphabet

bueno

good

presenta

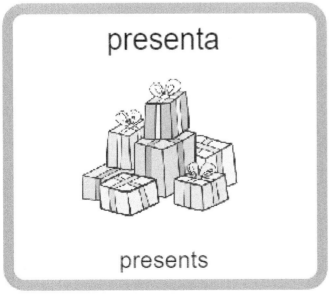

presents

noticias

news

pollo

chicken

caracol

snail

chorizo

sausage

sapo

toad

pregunta

question

lápiz labial

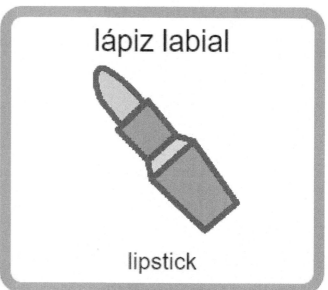

lipstick

triste

sad

cero

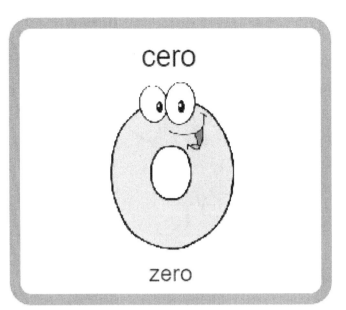

zero

reunirse

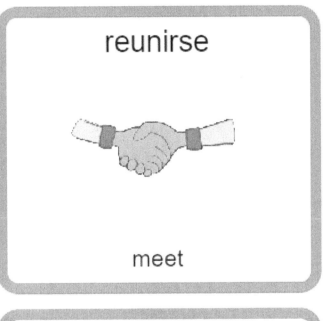

meet

escritura

writing

peluca

wig

regalos

gifts

frijol

bean

iglú

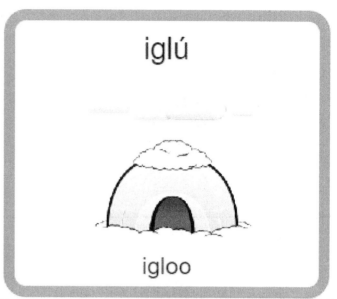

igloo

toalla

towel

coala

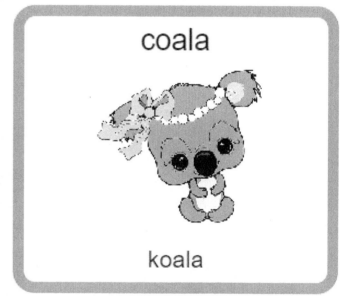

koala

mochila

backpack

sirena

mermaid

fútbol

soccer

hundimiento

sinking

unicornio

unicorn

que huele

smelling

sofá

sofa

paquete

package

zanahoria

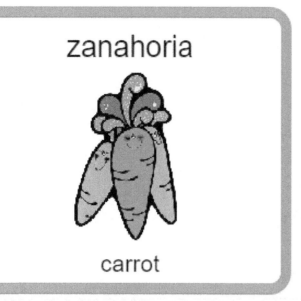

carrot

búho

owl

cabeza

head

soñoliento

sleepy

alfombra

carpet

mago

magician

yak

yak

beber

drink

pingüino

penguin

linterna

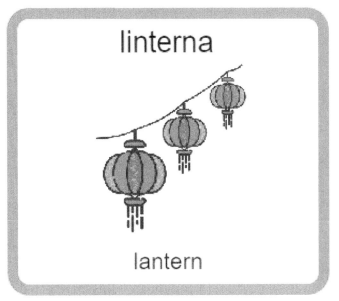

lantern

uva

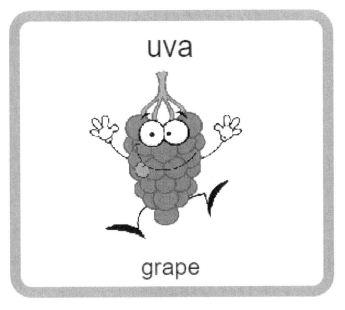

grape

paracaídas

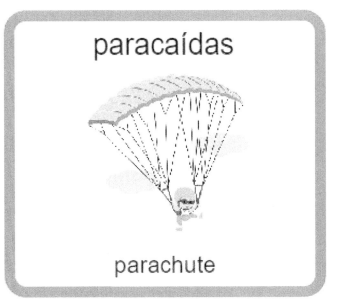

parachute

ordenadores

computer

morsa

walrus

whisky

whiskey

él

him

ojo

eyes

empanadas

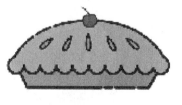

pie

bebé

baby

hueso

bone

lentes

glass

limpiando

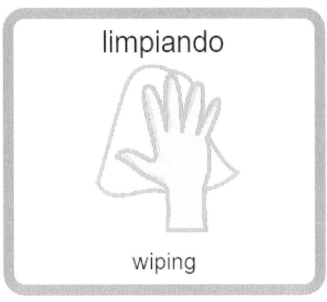

wiping

cuenco

bowl

hospital

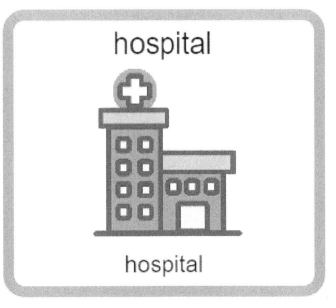

hospital

tejer

knitting

arriba

up

dos

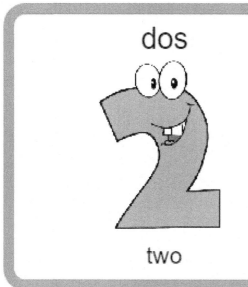

two

peras

pear

conducción

driving

vegetales

vegetable

lanzamiento

throwing

delicioso

delicious

microscopio

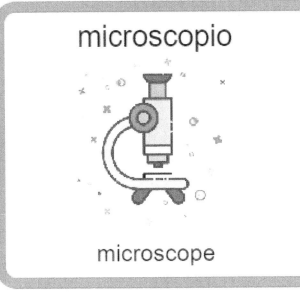

microscope

hola

hello

peine

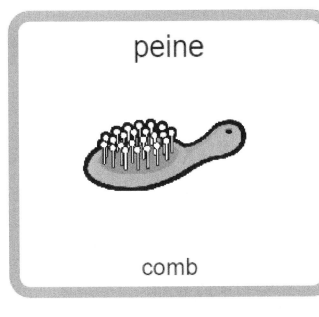

comb

pistola

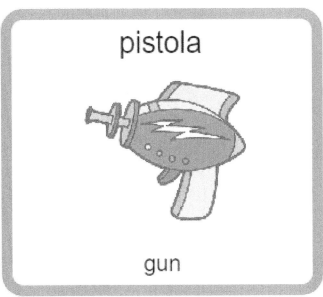

gun

ducharse

showering

otoño

fall

cavar

dig

autobús

bus

nieve

snow

leyendo

reading

medicina

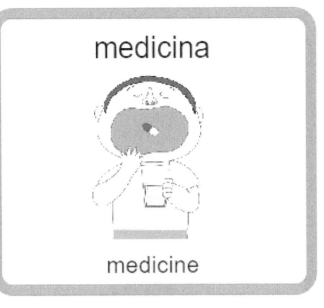

medicine

gerente

manager

castillo

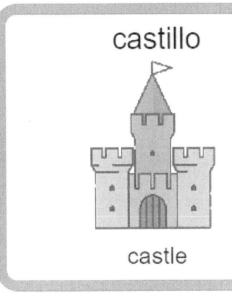

castle

pastel

cake

paraguas

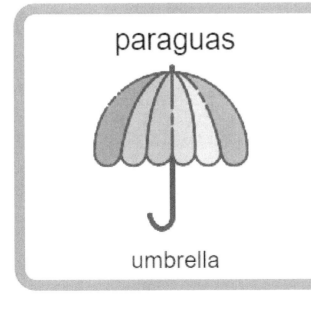

umbrella

piernas

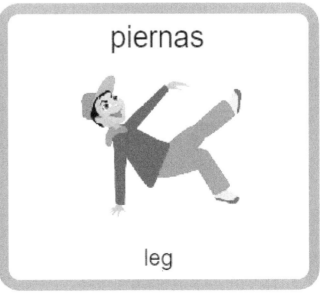

leg

zorro

fox

gusano

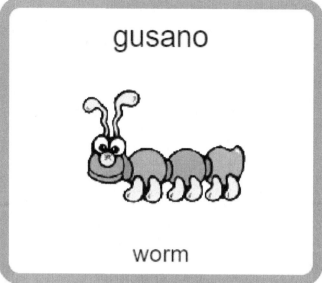

worm

pares

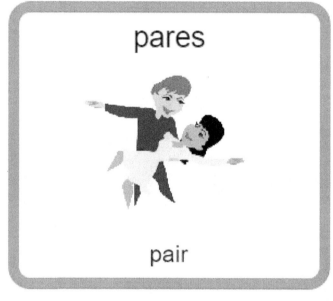

pair

polvo

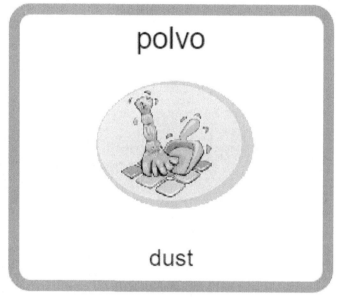

dust

picar

nibble

regla

ruler

sesos

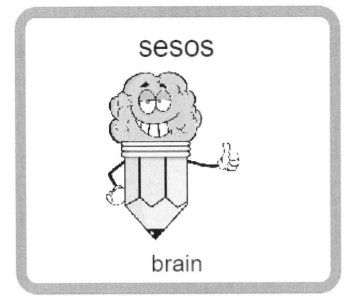

brain

animales

animals

granjero

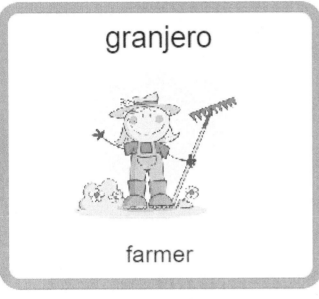

farmer

ciencia

science

fuerte

strong

licuadora

blender

león

lion

siesta

nap

boxeo

boxing

plantas

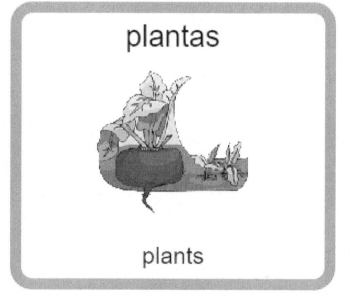

plants

cortador

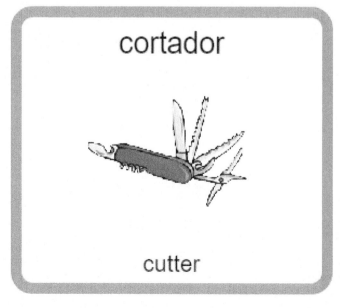

cutter

cuello

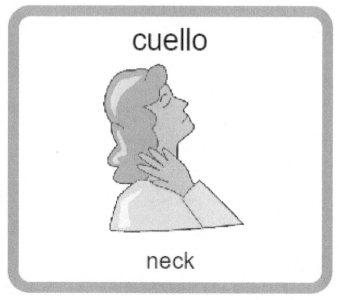

neck

hermano

brother

pájaro

bird

día

day

policía

policeman

prohibir

forbid

hilo

yarn

circulo

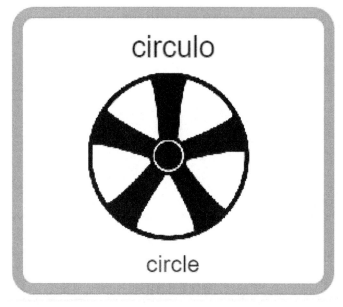

circle

detener

stop

coco

coconut

cuchillo

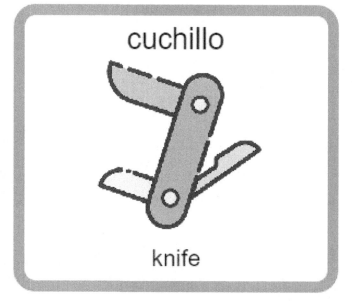

knife

nabo

turnip

suelo

ground

oval

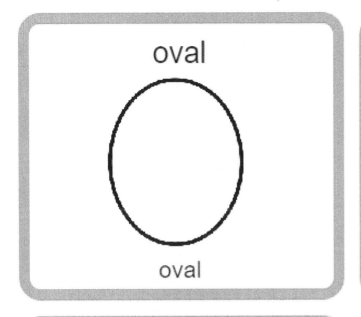

oval

princesa

princess

sangre

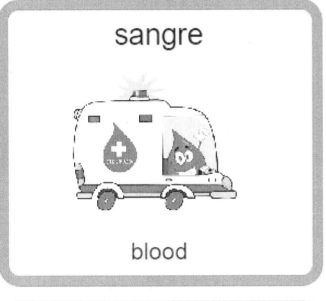

blood

ratones

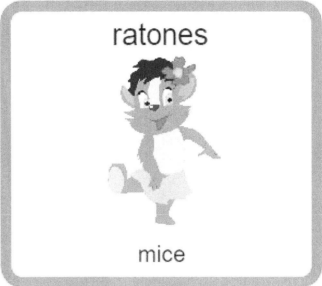

mice

un pan

bread

vendaje

dressing

maleta

suitcase

elefante

elephant

estacas

peg

limón

lemon

frambuesa

raspberry

niño

boy

oso

bear

aburrido

bored

bombilla

lightbulb

radio

radio

maceta

pot

amor

love

codorniz

quail

dom

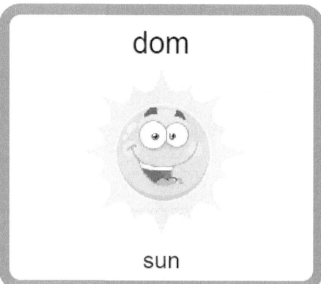

sun

gallina

hen

disfrutar

enjoy

mates

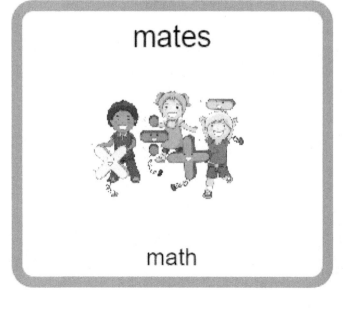

math

aguacate

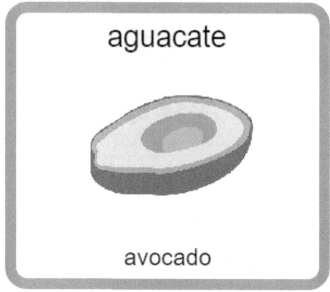

avocado

cebolla

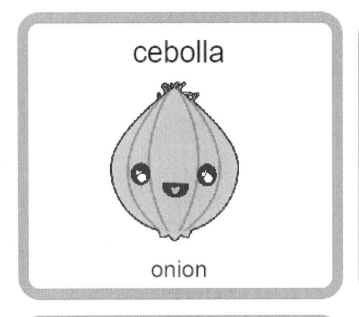

onion

silla

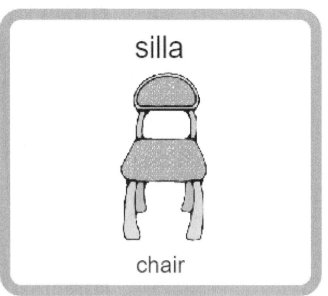

chair

brazo

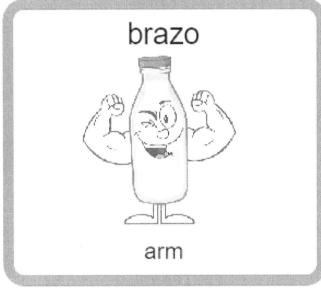

arm

zapatos

shoes

enfermera

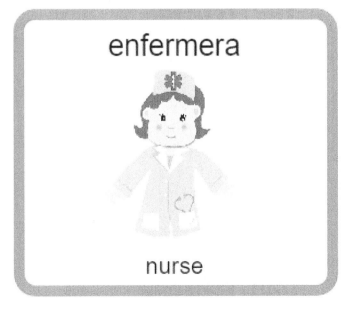

nurse

rana

frog

monstruo

monster

cabra

goat

puerco espín

porcupine

tapas

lid

guantes

glove

brocha
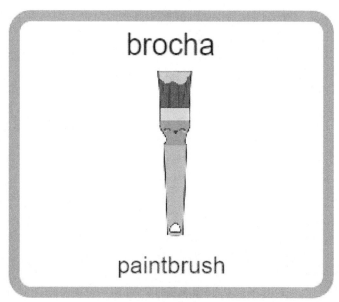
paintbrush

papelera

bin

puerta

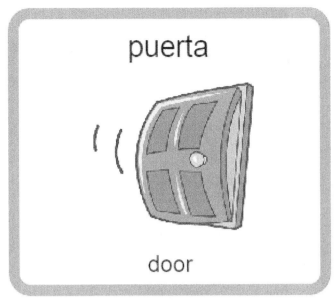

door

huevos

egg

camello

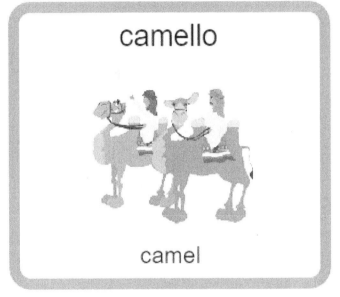

camel

cocinero

chef

pollitos

chick

gato

cat

fábrica

factory

papá

dad

esconder

hide

nariz
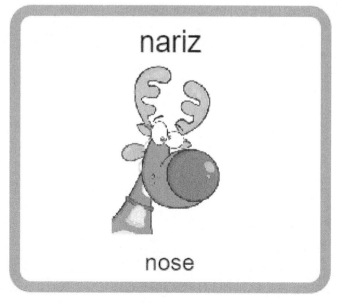
nose

aplaudir

clap

oveja

sheep

nombre

name

poderoso

powerful

café

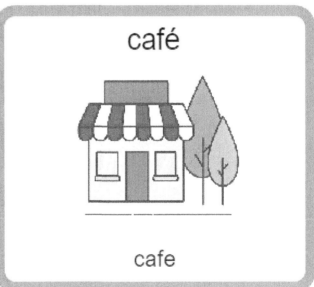

cafe

ruidoso

loud

ancla

anchor

martillo

hammer

tortuga

turtle

lengua

tongue

vaquero

cowboy

pomelo

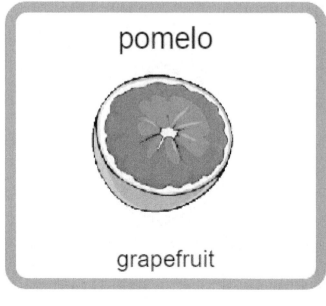

grapefruit

mojado

wet

panda

panda

sopa

soup

correr

run

ostra

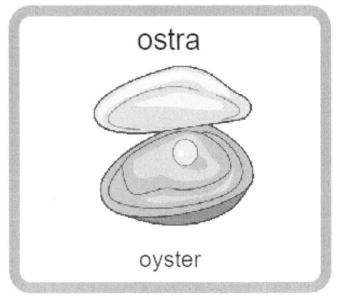

oyster

jeringuilla

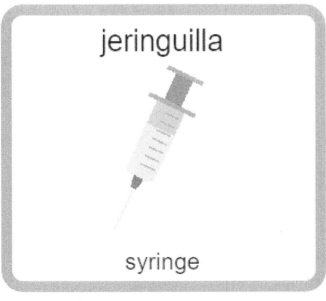

syringe

camioneta

van

vestidos

dress

bola

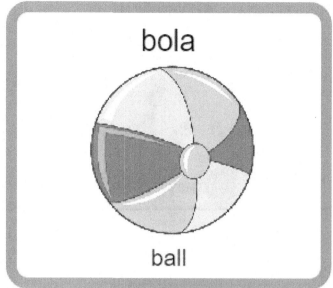

ball

basura

trash

árbol

tree

fotógrafo

photographer

sofá

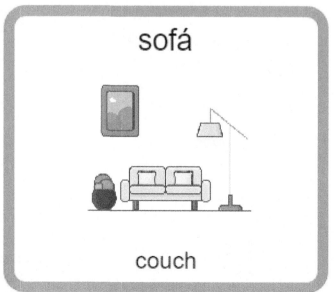

couch

mensaje

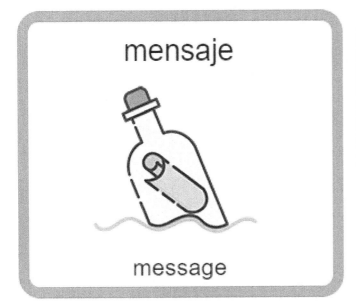

message

helado

ice cream

policía

cop

viento

wind

cola

tail

rastrillo

rake

aleta

fin

bote

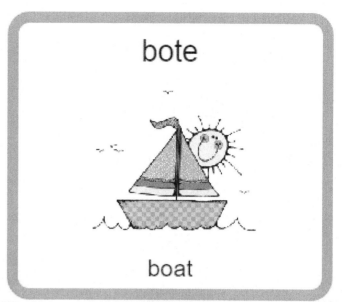

boat

carretilla

barrow

bicicleta

bike

palas

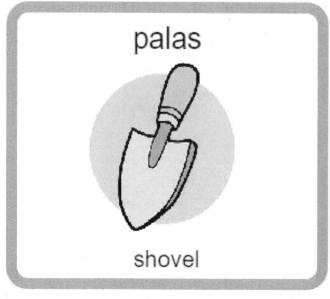

shovel

cinco

five

volcán

volcano

tres

three

enojado

mad

doctor

doctor

paloma

pigeon

bosquejo

sketch

de miedo

scary

baloncesto

basketball

disminución

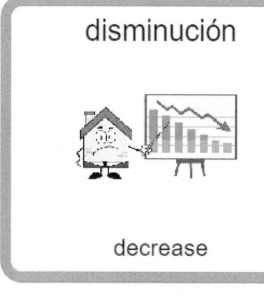

decrease

juegos

game

perrito

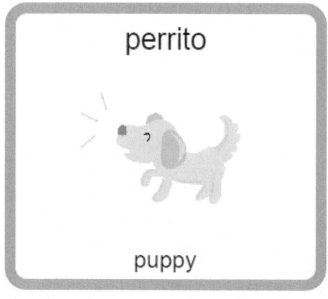

puppy

queso

cheese

patata

potato

limpiar

clean

tijeras

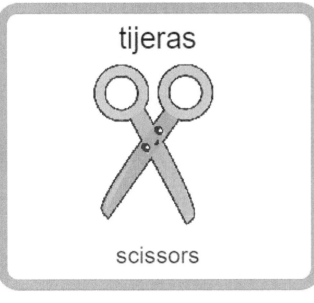

scissors

escalera

ladder

los niños

kids

serpiente

snake

muñeca

doll

despierta

wake up

refugios

shelter

seis

six

hockey

hockey

iglesia

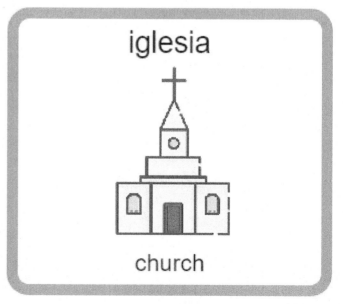

church

tomate

tomato

berenjenas

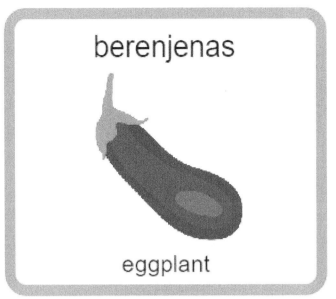

eggplant

cactus

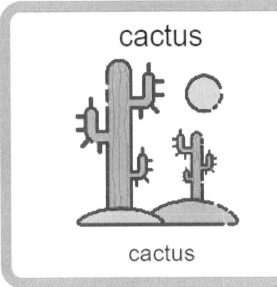

cactus

golf

golf

examen

quiz

pegamento

glue

cachorro

cub

sándwiches

sandwich

comer

eat

sonar

sound

montañas

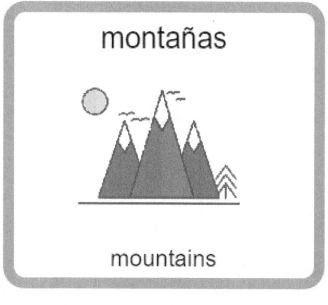

mountains

imagen

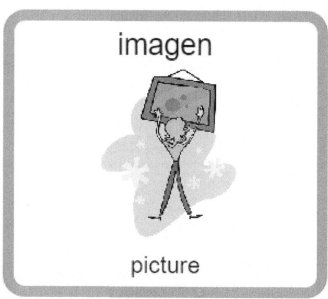

picture

lavar

wash

botas

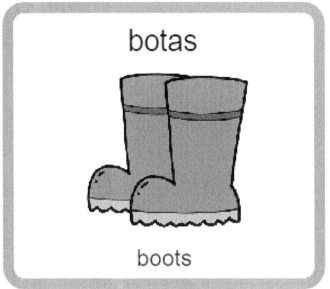

boots

siete

seven

mono

monkey

vaca

cow

dedo

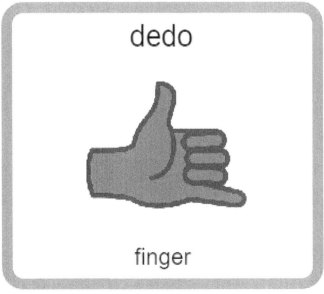

finger

tazas

mug

mucama

maid

museo

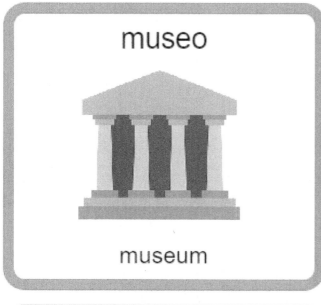

museum

jaula

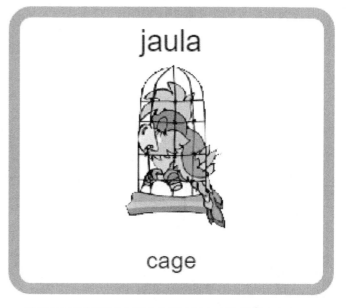

cage

perlas

pearls

canguro

kangaroo

cisne

swan

brújula

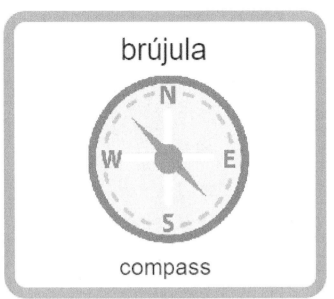

compass

orejas

ears

seta

mushroom

pelícano

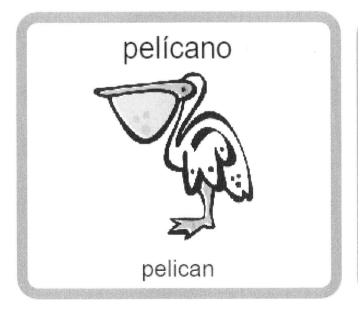

pelican

ángel

angel

madera

wood

antorcha

torch

nadando

swimming

aptitud

fitness

diente

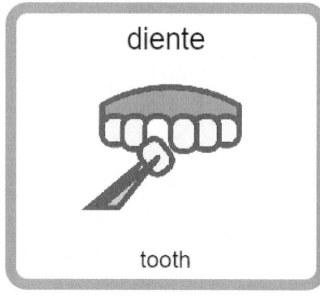

tooth

pagoda

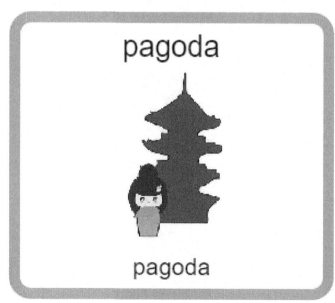

pagoda

canto

singing

pescar

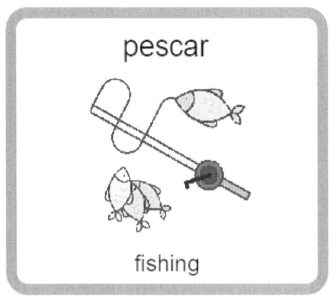

fishing

rata

rat

político

politician

tetera

teapot

boda

wedding

chocolate

chocolate

campana

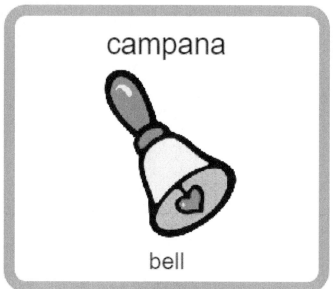

bell

águila

eagle

fresco

fresh

ballon

ballon

botella

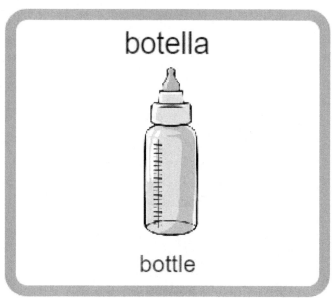

bottle

caballero

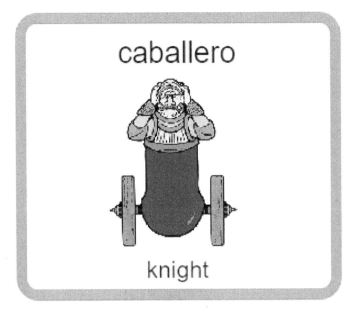

knight

loro

parrot

rey

king

avión

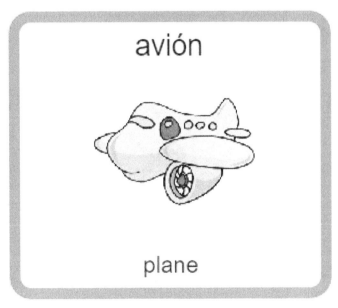

plane

niñito

toddler

hierba

grass

tirando

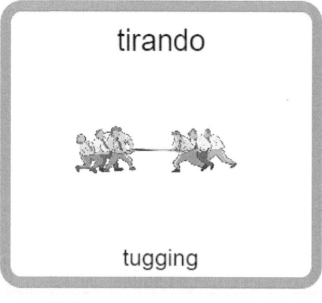

tugging

alegre

joyful

insecto

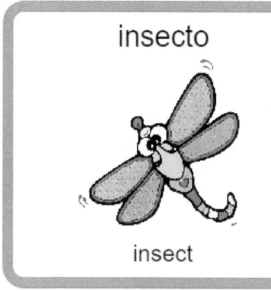

insect

camiones

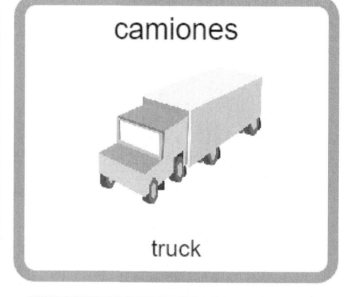

truck

maíz

corn

miel

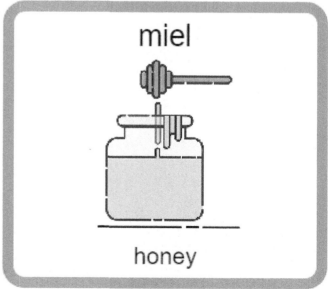

honey

verano

summer

smoking

tuxedo

babero

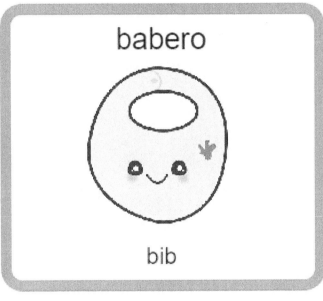

bib

sentar

sit

mordedura

bite

vagón

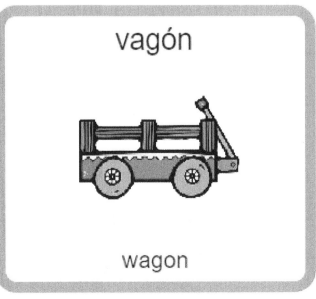

wagon

cerca

fence

lápices de color

crayons

compras

shopping

dientes

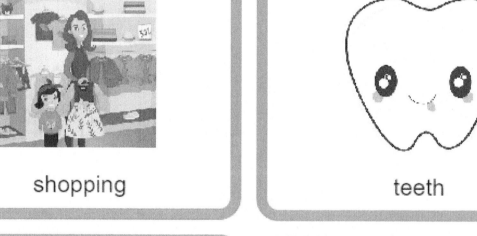

teeth

domar

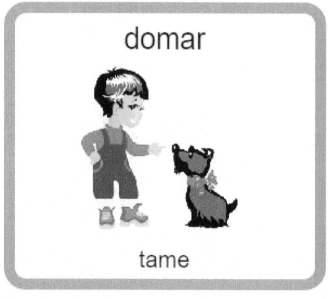

tame

yogur

yogurt

infeliz

unhappy

barbilla

chin

chaleco

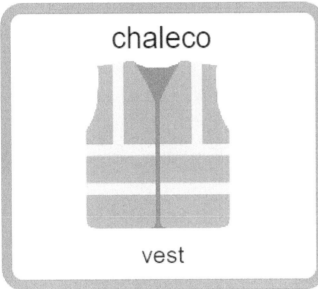

vest

tímido

shy

ventana

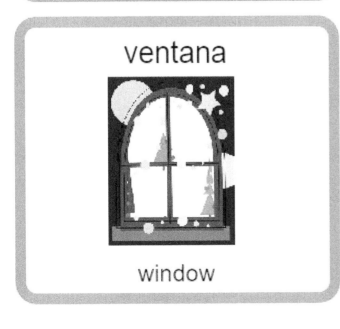

window

premios

prize

Made in the USA
Las Vegas, NV
13 June 2021